BRITAIN IN OLD PHOTOGRAPHS

DURHAM AT WORK

MICHAEL F. RICHARDSON

ALAN SUTTON PUBLISHING LIMITED

Alan Sutton Publishing Limited
Phoenix Mill · Far Thrupp · Stroud
Gloucestershire · GL5 2BU

COUNTY
DURHAM
BOOKS

British Library Cataloguing in Publication Data.
A catalogue record for this book is available from
the British Library.

ISBN 0-7509-0988-9

First published 1995

Cover photographs: (front) the launch of the
Dunelm, Brown's Boathouse, 1911; (back) the
final touches being put to the Royal Festival
Hall organ, by J. Prested (left) and J. A.
Newton, 1954.

Typeset in 9/10 Sabon.
Typesetting and origination by
Alan Sutton Publishing Limited.
Printed in Great Britain by
WBC, Bridgend, Mid Glam.

Contents

Mrs Elizabeth Eltringham from the Queen's Head Yard, Back Silver Street, *c.* 1932. She is seen here doing the family washing with her poss-stick and tub. A reminder of the good old days!

Introduction

The city and diocese of Durham have chosen 1995 to celebrate the millennium of their foundation because it is 1,000 years since the monks from Lindisfarne brought the body of St Cuthbert to Durham. We know, however, that there was a Roman settlement at Old Durham and an ancient hill fort at Maiden Castle, just outside the modern city.

Today the city of Durham is increasingly concerned with ecclesiastical and educational matters. The buildings round Palace Green – the Norman castle and the Romanesque cathedral at opposite sides – were declared a World Heritage site by UNESCO in 1987. The university, founded in 1832 by Bishop Van Mildert – the last of the Prince Bishops – is expanding, with a college at Stockton, and special relations with Teikyo University in Japan.

At the time of the beginning of photography, the city had just acquired a main line railway and a remarkable viaduct, of which an unusual early picture is included in this book. An achievement of Victorian engineering often underrated, the viaduct deployed some 21,300 ft of oak pilings, for it was built on sand, yet had a span of 832 ft. It is from the viaduct, built in 1855–7, that most people have their first view of Durham City, set in the hollow below, within the famous loop of the River Wear.

The population of 14,088 recorded in the 1851 census – just over half that of the city today – included 898 Irish people, almost all brought to the north-east by employment on the construction of the railways. Ten years before, the census showed the existence of 913 domestic servants in a population of 13,188, an indication of the middle-class nature of the city. In 1851, as many as 308 people had jobs in agriculture, for the city retained close connections with its rural hinterland, as several of Michael Richardson's photographs demonstrate; I particularly like the picture of the farm hind (see page 59).

The two main industries within Durham City in the late nineteenth and twentieth centuries were carpet weaving and organ building. There were in the city itself several coalmines, none large, and from 1871 Durham was the scene of the Miners' Gala, which became world famous. Coalmining, however, was a major occupation of the county rather than of the city. In 1851, 201 males and 32 females were involved in carpet weaving, a seventh of them children under the age of fourteen. The weavers, many of whom had come in from other weaving districts, lived mostly in Back Lane, to the north of St Nicholas' Church which dominates Durham's Market Place. The carpet factory by the River Wear dated from 1814, and was known as Henderson's under three generations of that family until its sale to Crossleys of Halifax in 1903, with the loss of over 300 jobs. Fortunately, a workman at the factory leased buildings and machinery from the Hendersons, and rebuilt the factory's fortunes as Hugh Mackay's. The resulting company received the Royal Warrant in 1972, three years after an arson attack destroyed the works and caused the removal to a site at Dragonville on the eastern outskirts of the city.

Harrison & Harrison Ltd, organ builders, began only in 1872 when the Revd Dr J.B. Dykes persuaded Thomas Harrison to remove from Rochdale; Thomas was shortly joined by his brother James. An old paper mill, in what is now Hawthorn Terrace, was purchased, and this was enlarged; the business is still conducted on the same site. Harrison organs are to be found all over the world, in cathedrals especially; the firm has an enviable reputation for restoring historic organs, including its own earlier models.

The most important industrial establishment in the neighbourhood of Durham in about 1900, however, was the Grange Iron Co. which leased the site of Grange Colliery at Carrville, just over two miles from the city centre, from the Marquis of Londonderry in 1866. The works covered some ten acres and constituted a township in their own right, for dwellings were created for the considerable workforce. In 1887 the company was awarded two silver medals and a bronze at the Royal Exhibition at Newcastle for compound air-compressing engines, air locomotives for underground haulage, and for colliery jigging screens. Its products were regularly exported.

Michael Richardson's photographs are rich in business interest. One of the Durham families long established in local enterprises was the Colpitts family. The grandfather ran stagecoaches with his brothers between Durham and Newcastle and Durham and Sunderland. The father opened the City Hotel in 1883. The brothers T. and H.C. Colpitts owned the Criterion Hotel from 1899. This was a favourite rendezvous for sportsmen, specializing in a blend of Scotch whisky in two strengths. J. and G. Archibald, owners of iron stores in Sunderland, in 1910 bought the business of T.J. Tomlinsons. Founded in 1840, the business had moved to a large warehouse at Gilesgate goods station in 1884. The Archibalds gave their name to a business with much more diversification in building materials when they sold to William McIntyre in 1924; the firm, greatly changed though it is, still flourishes. One of the more noticeable buildings in the city with a tall chimney, at the junction of Atherton Street and North Road, was used at the end of the nineteenth century as the premises of Geo. Hauxwell and Sons, Iron and Brass Founders. Many drain covers and grates in the city bear the name to this day.

Michael Richardson's photographs recall for us a variety of tradesmen and professionals, such as the Edis family of photographers; Joseph Brown the boat builder (Durham is the northern home of the modern racing-boat); the Gradon family of builders and timber merchants who produced two mayors of the city in 1875 and 1916; the Goodyears, who had one of the largest building and contracting businesses in the north-east (F.W. Goodyear was mayor twice, in 1916 and 1926); the McCartans, father and son, who were linen manufacturers and merchants in Gilesgate and had a branch in Dromara, Co. Down; and Ralph Charlton, wholesale and retail draper of Claypath, who had spacious showrooms and millinery workrooms on the premises.

One of the rarer pictures shows Sherburn Hospital Chapel after the disastrous fire of 1864. Another evocative photograph is of Christmas Day at the Union Workhouse, later St Margaret's Hospital. Life in Durham was often not easy for young or old. Walter Shea, who spent his life in the service of Mackay's, has recorded his early days: 'Times were really hard; the school leaving age was fourteen but lots of children started work long before that, usually working nights, Saturdays and school holidays, as delivery boys. I started work as a delivery boy for a butcher in Claypath. I worked about one hour in the morning before school then an hour or so after school, and all day on Saturday, for which I was paid 2s 6d. This was in 1916. My father, who was a weaver at Hugh Mackay's, seldom had a full week's work, except at certain times of the year.'

Even people in full employment in the north-east received relatively low wages. In 1877 the staff of Harrison & Harrison, twenty-three of them, enjoyed total wages of £33 12s 8d per week; craftsmen earned only between £1 7s and £2 10s 6d. In 1901, the wages bill at the organ-makers with fifty-six staff was still only £104 3s ½d. Arthur and Harry Harrison, who ran the business, drew only £3 each a week and their retired father £10. Nationally, wages were some 80 per cent higher in 1900 than in 1860 and living standards had improved, though in many areas – including Durham – not housing conditions. Wages were comparatively static between the world wars, and real economic improvement came only after 1939. Moreover, unemployment was an endemic feature of north-east life for whole generations.

Everyone will find something in this book which will intrigue them about the past in an area which arouses such loyalty in its people. For some, the photographs will be reminders of good old days; for others a record of past suffering. All will feel a debt to Michael Richardson and those who have contributed their photographs to his collection for stirring up memories, whether glad or sad.

Professor G.R. Batho
Durham 1995

BUSINESSES

Aitchisons grocer's shop, 1 Alexandria Crescent,
c. 1905. The shop was later run by Mr T.
Robertson. More recently the property has been
used by Durham School.

John Reed Edis, the famous Durham photographer, photographed by his daughter Daisy, *c.* 1937. John Edis was born at Tottenham Court Road in 1861 and was proud of the fact that he was a Londoner. After training at the newly formed London Polytechnic he worked with his uncle, who had a photography business in the Strand. He then came north in 1883 and worked at Darlington, where he married, before moving to Durham in 1890. There he joined Fred Morgan. He soon branched out for himself, first at 27 Sherburn Road and later at 53 Saddler Street, moving to 52 Saddler Street *c.* 1898. During the First World War John served as a special constable in the city.

Daisy Edis photographed by her father, c. 1903. Daisy started working with her father at the age of fifteen. She went on to become an artist in her own right, her portraits being exhibited as far away as Japan and America. She married George Spence, but continued to use her maiden name until she died in 1964. She is buried in St Giles' 1927 churchyard.

Daisy's son, John Edis Spence, photographed by Daisy in about 1927. This portrait was exhibited at the International Exhibition at Ohio, USA in 1933, and was titled 'My Son'. It won an Award of Merit. John became a naval chaplain and later an Honorary Canon of Truro Cathedral.

Mary Wilkinson in period costume, an exhibition photograph by Daisy Edis, 1920s. Mary was a re-toucher for Edis's all her working life.

The Edis Studio, 52 Saddler Street, 1920s. These premises are now the offices for the British School of Motoring. John Edis opened the studio here in about 1898. The premises had previously belonged to a Miss Brewster, who was listed as a fancy hair-worker in *The Durham Directory* of 1897.

Harrington's mobile kitchen at the top of Station Lane, 1890s. Joseph Harrington, pictured in the centre, was a shoe and clogmaker of 181 Gilesgate. He sold takeaway food from his mobile kitchen in the evenings in Durham Market Place.

Harrington's Tea Tent on the Racecourse for the Miners' Gala, 1890s.

Miss Emma Jarvis outside her tobacconist's shop, 2 Old Elvet, June 1911. The shop was decorated for the coronation of King George and Queen Mary. This is one of four identical shops which were built in about 1905. The site had previously been that of the Durham City Working Men's Club, originally the Wheatsheaf Inn (see page 95).

The corner of Old Elvet showing 1 Old Elvet, which was Hayton's newsagents, *c.* 1910. The property is now an off-licence. The properties to the left of Hayton's are the four small retail shops which replaced the Durham City Working Men's Club.

Durham County Hospital, August 1933. The hospital was built in about 1849–50 at a cost of £7,518 14*s* 10*d*, in the Elizabethan style. Much of the old building still survives, but has been hidden by modern extensions. It is now a psychiatric hospital.

Christmas Day at the workhouse, Crossgate, *c.* 1924. The workhouse was built in 1837, and was known as the Union Workhouse. When built it contained ten rooms as sleeping apartments and a dining hall, which also served as a chapel. The workhouse was capable of containing 150 inmates. It is now being altered for student accommodation for St John's College after many years as St Margaret's Geriatric Hospital.

Old Durham Fever Hospital, *c.* 1918. The hospital was situated near the site of the old Shincliffe Mill, now part of the Shincliffe Mill Boarding Kennels. The hospital was erected in 1910. Back row, second from the left, is Matthew Clarkson. The isolation period was approximately six weeks.

Ramsbottom's pork butchers, 106 Claypath, *c.* 1910. The shop stood below what is now Boots the Chemists opposite St Nicholas' Church. It later became Fred Robinson's (see below).

Fred Robinson's pork butchers, 106 Claypath, *c.* 1954. The shop was demolished in the 1960s. Miss Jean Reed is seen standing in the doorway. To the left of the shop was the King's Arms Hotel.

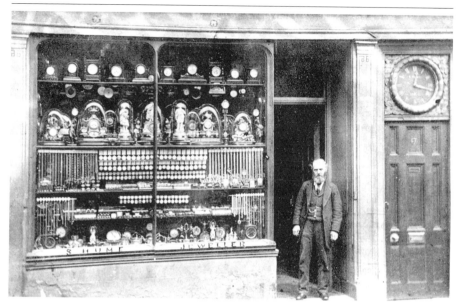

Samuel Hume, jeweller and clock maker, 17 Elvet Bridge, *c.* 1890. Samuel originated from Glanton, Northumberland, and first started business in Houghton-le-Spring before coming to Gilesgate in 1861. He later moved to the premises of the late John Crudas & Son, 17 Elvet Bridge. He died in 1909, and the business was carried on by his son-in-law Walter Holdsworth until 1923, when the business moved to 1 North Road.

S. Hume, jeweller, 1 North Road, *c.* 1923. Walter Holdsworth (on the left) with George R. Middlemass, a watch and clock repairer in his employ. The shop became Alexander's around 1927, and more recently it was called In Time.

Mr W.A. Bramwell, jeweller, 24 Elvet Bridge, *c.* 1929. Mr Bramwell was a keen photographer and a member of Durham City Camera Club; it is thanks to him that many scenes from Durham's past have been preserved. Many of the slides the late Dr Gibby (1902–89) used for his well-loved talks on Durham history were originally taken by Mr Bramwell.

The Eclipse wallpaper shop, 9 Saddler Street, c. 1929. The shop stood opposite Magdalene Steps. It is now a kitchenware shop.

Maynards Ltd, confectioners, 8 Saddler Street, 1929. The shop window display is for the Miners' Gala. Maynards had a number of shops in the city. This shop is now the Scholl Shoe Shop, opposite Magdalene Steps. The girl on the right is Grace Adams.

Mrs Hughes, 38 Gilesgate, Durham's last straw mattress maker, *c.* 1920. The property stood to the left of the old Drill Hall at the bottom of Gilesgate Bank.

Mr Robert Burns Wilkinson pictured on the right, with his nephew George Elgey, outside the general dealers' shop which he ran with his wife. It stood at the bottom of Gilesgate Bank left of Moody's Buildings, in the 1930s (see page 42 for a photograph of Mrs Wilkinson, his wife).

Porter's Stores, 43 Gilesgate, *c.* 1910. Standing in the doorway is Joseph Francis Porter. Porter's was an old-established firm which started up in about 1861. It also had a shop in North Road, where the electricity showrooms are now. The premises at Gilesgate stood to the right of the old Drill Hall and were later used by Cowies' Motor Cycles as a showroom. They were demolished in about 1967 for the new through road and Gilesgate roundabout.

Robert J. Maddison, general dealers, 201 Gilesgate, *c.* 1890. The photograph was taken by Obadiah Woodcock, a photographer from 193 Gilesgate. The shop is now a private house, and stands approximately opposite the Woodman Inn, Gilesgate.

A group of painters pictured in Durham Indoor Market, in the early 1900s. On the right of the front row is Isaac Arckless from 2 Wanless Terrace. The photograph shows some of the butchers' stands in the background with the hooks for hanging meat.

Lockerbie's shoeing forge, 111 Gilesgate, *c.* 1904. The forge stood behind the old Bay Horse public house, now rebuilt and called the Durham Light Infantryman.

Ice-cream carts belonging to the Dimambro family, *c.* 1911. The building on the left is part of Maynards Row. This area was demolished in the late 1940s to make the new entrance for the Gilesgate Community Centre (Vane Tempest Hall).

Durham City postmen, 1920s. The uniforms have an American Civil War look about them. The old post office, now a licensed betting shop, stood in Saddler Street. The post office moved to Claypath in 1929 and, more recently, to Albert House, Silver Street.

Builders working on the construction of the Cottage Homes, Crossgate Moor, built by Ainsley Brothers of Durham, 1926. On the far right of the front row, standing, is Fred Hinsley. The Cottage Homes were officially opened by the Durham Board of Guardians on 26 March 1927. They now belong to the Durham Johnston Comprehensive School.

The founder of Wood & Watson's Mineral Water Works, William Henry Wood, pictured when he was Mayor of the City, 1919. He was also Mayor in 1909. A well-known Freemason, William Wood died in 1924 and a fine granite tombstone marks his grave in St Giles' 1870 churchyard. The business of W.H. Wood was established in about 1890, and he was later joined by Mr Joseph Watson, his brother-in-law. Mr Watson retired from the partnership just before the start of the First World War.

The old office of Wood & Watson's Ltd, 132 Gilesgate, *c*. 1960. The site previously belonged to Child's Tannery. The building was demolished and rebuilt in about 1960. To the left of the photograph is the lane leading down to the Silver Link footbridge and Pelaw Woods.

The loading bay for the wagons at Wood & Watson's, November 1947. This photograph shows the new bottle crates, which were bakelite and aluminium. These were not successful and the firm soon reverted to using the old-fashioned wooden crates. Standing on the wagon is Vic Richardson, one of the drivers.

Half of the staff from the Durham City Provincial Laundry, Providence Row, 1937. Back row, left to right: Nelly Crossman, Joan Egan, Kitty Burns, Hilda Robinson, Gladys Soulsby, Florrie Pattison. Middle row: Mary Shiell, Margaret Mortimer, Olive Akenhead, Ethel Whale, Violet Wills, Nora Stainsley, Peggy Forster, Lydia Adamson, Thomasina Redden. Front row: Mary Cooper, Elsie Crow, Edith Brown, Doris West, Betty Proud, Rene Clark. Seated: Evelyn Bell, Nora Liddle.

Edwin Oliver, tobacconist, 82 North Road, *c*. 1920. The shop window advertises Procopides cigarettes, once a popular brand but now unknown.

R.A. Charlton, draper and milliner, 103 Claypath, 1913. Mr Ralph Charlton established the business in 1871 in conjunction with Messrs J. and R.A. Stokes; in 1884 the two Stokes retired, leaving Mr Charlton the sole proprietor. The instruments hanging above the windows reflected heat on customers looking in the shop windows.

William Rolling outside his fruit shop at 19a Sunderland Road near the present Edge Court, Gilesgate, *c.* 1933. Rolling later had a shop built on the opposite side of the road, now Alan's Hairdressers.

Johnson & Cosgrove, family grocers, 45 Gilesgate, 1935. The shop stood at the bottom of Gilesgate bank to the right of Station Lane. The premises had previously been William Bramley's fancy drapers. The property was demolished to make way for the new through road in about 1967.

John Oliver, fishmonger and curer, 131 Millburngate, c. 1950. The shop stood to the right of the Five Ways Inn, and is now Gregg's the bakers. The name John Oliver still survives at Oliver's shop, 57 Hawthorn Terrace, Durham City.

Mr John Oliver, the third generation of John Olivers serving in the fishmonger's shop, 131 Millburngate, c. 1950. The business was established in the 1880s. The previous shop stood over the road at 2 North Road.

Ballard's tobacconists, *c.* 1944. The shop stood to the right of Oliver's fishmongers, at 132 Millburngate. On the left is pictured Mrs Mary E. Ballard and on the right Carrie Coulson. The business later moved to the top of North Road.

The staff from Boots the Chemist, which also had a lending library, 29 Silver Street, 1947. The photograph was taken by Daisy Edis outside the almshouses on Palace Green.

Mr John Oliver (not of the same family as the fishmonger) with his fruit and vegetable cart at Teesdale Terrace, Gilesgate Moor, c. 1949. He is seen here selling bilberries to his sister, Mrs Elizabeth Brice.

Tommy Atkinson, the projectionist at the Rex Cinema, Gilesgate Moor, on the closing night, 18 January 1958. He is seen loading his last film, *The Eagle Squadron*, after sixteen years at the Rex. In that time he had seen almost five thousand films.

Mason's cash chemists, 69 Saddler Street, 1938. To the far left is Earl's the baker, famous for their pies, and to the right Harland's wet fish shop; the latter later became Macdonald's, and, in its final years, Peacock's. Waterstone's bookshop now occupies the site of the chemists. The ancient street name Fleshergate can be seen above the doorway on the extreme right of the picture.

Joseph William Pattison standing in the telegraph office on Elvet Bridge, *c.* 1897. Joseph went on to serve in the First World War (see page 109).

An advertisement for Colpitts wine and spirit merchants, 1 and 2 South Street, *c.* 1909.

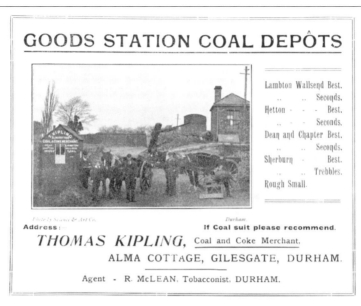

Kipling's coal yard, Gilesgate goods station, *c.* 1909. Kipling's was established in about 1889, and was one of the main suppliers of household coal to the city. Many residents will remember going to Kipling's coal yard where one could buy as little as a bucket of coal if there was a cash flow problem.

An advertisement showing the shop-front of J. Colven's, 21 Silver Street, *c.* 1909. The site is now a pizza restaurant at the bottom of Silver Street.

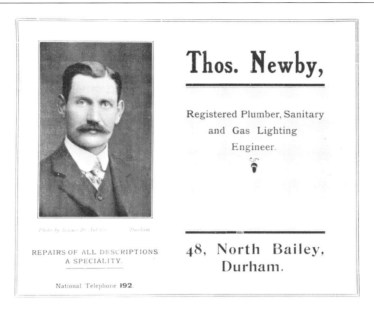

An interesting advertisement showing the portrait of Thomas Newby, plumber and gas lighting engineer to the Dean and Chapter, 48 North Bailey, *c.* 1909. At this time his work was in great demand, as the main source of lighting was gas.

Blackburn's cab business, at Dragon Villa, *c.* 1909. On the right can be seen their horse-drawn hearse.

Telephone Nº 128.
Telegrams,
"LOWES LTD., DURHAM."

ESTABLISHED 1857.

Address all letters to MARBLE WORKS, 180 GILESGATE.
DURHAM.

STONE, MARBLE & MONUMENTAL WORKS.

CHURCH WORK.
MURAL TABLETS, FONTS, ALTARS
PAVEMENTS.

SHOP & SHIP FITTINGS.
FISH, LAVATORY & SLATE SLABS,
URINALS, &c.

TURNED STONE & MARBLE.

KITCHEN RANGES & COOKERS,
REGISTER GRATES.
ENAMELLED TILES.
GLAZED SINKS.

CEMENT, PLASTER, HAIR, &c.

CONTRACTORS FOR
MARBLE, GRANITE, MOSAIC
AND TILE WORK.

COLOURED MARBLES
BEING MORE OR LESS
UNSOUND, ARE QUOTED FOR
SUBJECT TO BEING
STOPPED AND CRAMPED
AS MAY BE FOUND
NECESSARY IN THE
WORKING.

BOUGHT OF

JOHN LOWES & SONS

LIMITED

MARBLE & BUILDERS' MERCHANTS.

DIRECTORS
W. HENRY LOWES

A letterhead belonging to John Lowes & Sons, marble & builders' merchants, 180 Gilesgate, from the 1920s. The marble works was founded by John Lowes in 1857. The premises had previously been a fine town house with its own orchard. Lowes soon became a well-respected firm, receiving orders from as far away as Exeter in the south and Frazerburgh in Scotland. At one time Lowes was the only works using Frosterley Marble and Wolsingham Blue.

Lowes Marble Works yard, *c.* 1910, showing the large cutting machine which was still in use when the works closed in the early 1960s.

F.W. Goodyear's builders' van in their yard at the top of Claypath, on the left of the old General Gordon public house. Goodyear's started in about 1895. The old Palladium Cinema in Claypath and the Fighting Cocks public house, South Street, were built by this firm.

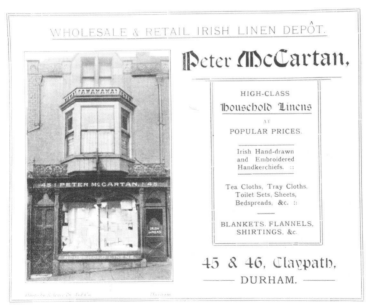

Peter McCartan's Irish Linen shop, 45 and 46 Claypath (now selling fishing tackle), c. 1909. Originally the business was established by Peter's father, Michael McCartan, in 1839. The old shop was situated at 1 and 2 Gilesgate, where the council flats, The Chains, now stand.

Mr Bob Dickinson (with beard) at his bookstall in Durham Indoor Market, 1970s. Mr Dickinson retired from the indoor market in 1993. He specialized in antiquarian books and books of local interest. He was also a lecturer in Classics at Durham University.

Archibald's showroom, Jagal House, at the bottom of Gilesgate Bank, 1938. The building had previously been St Giles' church hall. In its final years, before it was demolished in the early 1960s, it was Cowie's motor cycle showroom, which Tom Cowie characteristically named Earls Court.

Section Two

TRANSPORT

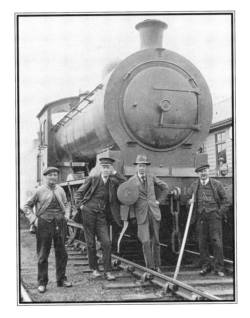

*Mr Harry Spraggon, second from the left,
stationmaster at Sherburn House station, 1927.
Mr Spraggon had worked at Sherburn House
station for fifty-four years. He began his service in
1874 as a telegraph boy. His father had been
stationmaster before him; together they rendered
106 years' service at Sherburn House station. The
locomotive standing in the station is a LNER Class
J27 freight engine.*

Sherburn House station, showing the south-bound platform, in the 1890s. Lines branched off to Old Durham Colliery and linked up with Shincliffe station and later Elvet station in 1893.

Sherburn House station, north-bound platform, 1920s. The station, a wooden construction, stood between West Sherburn and Sherburn Hospital. It closed in 1931.

The building of the railway embankment for the city viaduct, *c.* 1855. The light building in the centre is the newly built Union Workhouse, which later became St Margaret's Hospital. The walled lane to the left is Red Hills Lane, which passes the Miners' Hall.

The viaduct under construction, seen from the top of North Road, *c.* 1856, showing the wooden scaffolding which was first erected. The building on the right is the newly built Bridge Inn.

Railway staff at Durham station, during the 1880s. The stationmaster was John George Wright; he is seen on the back row, left of the centre column.

Here we see three women porters at Durham station, c. 1918. They were taking the place of men who, during the First World War, had been called to the front. The lady in the centre of the back row is Janet Wilkinson, wife of Robert Burns Wilkinson (see page 19).

The opening of Sherburn Viaduct, 20 July 1844. The viaduct stood south of Sherburn Village near Sherburn House Hospital. Sherburn House Beck ran underneath it. Later the viaduct was turned into an embankment. The cathedral can be seen to the right of centre.

A Sunderland to Durham train crossing Brasside (or Belmont) Viaduct, c. 1915. The viaduct was opened in 1844. It is no longer in use, but still stands proudly linking Belmont to Brasside.

Belmont Junction, also known as Auckland Junction, 1950s. The line on the right is leading off to Gilesgate goods station. It was here on 20 December 1921 that an express locomotive travelling from Aberdeen to Penzance with eleven coaches crashed into four standing coaches which were being shunted to a siding; fortunately no one was killed.

The Aberdeen to Penzance express locomotive Class Z 4–4–2 No. 720, lying on its side at Belmont Junction the day after the crash, 21 December 1921. Owing to alterations on the main line at Langley Bridge all rail traffic was diverted via Leamside.

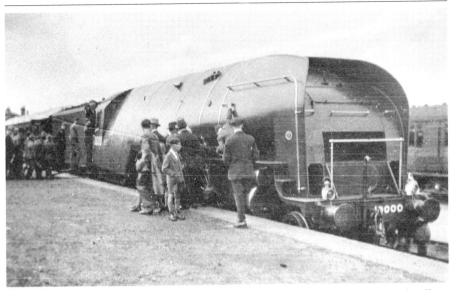

The Hush Hush at Elvet station, Sunday 6 July 1930. The delight of every schoolboy, this type 4–6–4 locomotive was built at Darlington in 1929. It was the first of its kind, with a water-tube boiler patented by H.E. Yarrow and Nigel Gresley, the LNER's Chief Mechanical Engineer. Its appearance was described as a whale-like casing painted in battleship grey with stainless steel bands. Its registration number was 10,000.

Sherburn Hill Colliery engine 'Monty', 1959. Monty was an ex-War Department type 0–6–0 saddle tank. The locomotive worked the line between Sherburn Hill Colliery and Sherburn Village coal sidings. Monty became a well-known sight, especially with the children. He was painted in deep red. When Sherburn Hill Colliery closed in August 1965 he was transferred to Horden Colliery, where he was cut up in 1974.

The old engine sheds belonging to Shincliffe station, *c.* 1960. The station opened on 28 June 1839 and closed in 1893 when Elvet station was opened. It became a council depot, and in recent years the site has been transformed into private housing and renamed The Mews.

Mr John W. Blackburn with one of the heavy horses outside his father's stables at Dragon Villa during the 1890s (see page 35 for his father's business advertisement).

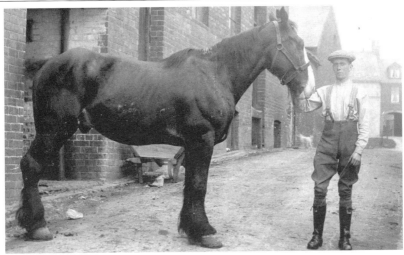

Mr Frank Fowler outside the stables at Wood & Watson's Ltd, Gilesgate, *c.* 1925. A terrible fire had occurred at the old stables on the night of 30 June 1901. Police Sergeant Hall and PC Robson were on duty at the Causeway Foot at the bottom of Gilesgate Bank, when they observed a red glow in the direction of W.H. Wood's Mineral Water Works. Upon reaching the site they discovered the stables on fire. They broke down the door and tried to rescue the horses. Out of the twenty horses stabled there twelve were saved. Damage was estimated at £600.

Mr George Rolling outside the Co-op Stables, behind the store at 7 Claypath, *c.* 1910. Mr Rolling was a driver with the store. He later set up in business by himself (see page 28 for a photograph of his first shop and his son William).

Mr R.W. Dixon, 81 Framwellgate, with his furniture removal wagon, early 1900s. In those days it was possible to move the whole household contents in one load.

The Durham Hand Laundry cart, of 60 Claypath, standing near the New Inn at the top of Church Street, *c.* 1912. Most of the work was from the middle classes in the city and from students at the university.

Wood & Watson's cart at Brancepeth village, standing outside the village school, *c.* 1925. Wood & Watson's delivered to all the mining villages on the outskirts of the city.

McKenzies, coal dealer and general carter, 77 Claypath, *c.* 1912. This horse and cart were entered in the Durham City Horse Parade at the Barracks, Vane Tempest Hall. The sacks on the cart probably contained household coal.

William Hockin, oil and egg merchant, from Surprise Cottage, Sherburn Road, *c.* 1910. This was a Horse Parade entrant at the Barracks. The trade constituted an odd combination – the oil would be lamp oil.

Mrs Jessie Layfield, seen here with Rington's Tea Cart at the top of Hallgarth Street near Mount Joy Crescent, *c.* 1929. Ringtons continues to be a household name in the region.

A young boy from the Bell's Ville area, Gilesgate Moor, with his cart advertising 'Light Carting Done', late 1940s. The building on the left is the rear of the old Hare & Hounds public house.

Joseph Johnson's 16 horsepower wagon from the City Brewery, 74 New Elvet, seen here outside the National Westminster Bank, Market Place, July 1916. The founder lived in Hallgarth Street from 1867 until 1884. The firm also had a branch at South Shields.

Missings' banana wagon from Station Lane, Gilesgate, dressed up for the Carnival Parade, *c.* 1923. It was quite common to find tropical spiders, occasionally alive, in their banana boxes. The young boys have their faces blacked; the driver is Sammy Burdon. The photograph was taken outside 129 Gilesgate at the Duck Pond (Gilesgate Green).

Mawson, Swan & Co., yeast and egg merchants, 115a Gilesgate, 1950s. The wagon fleet is seen here in the courtyard, where Armstrong's Cycles now have a shop

Fowler & Armstrong's garage, 74 New Elvet, *c.* 1926. In about 1921 Messrs W.A. Armstrong and M. Fowler, auctioneer and valuer, formed the business Fowler & Armstrong. They specialized in spare parts, and were the sole agents in the Durham area for Austin, Morris and Wolseley cars. In 1926 the firm purchased part of the disused premises of Joseph Johnson's brewery.

The new garage of Fowler & Armstrong, New Elvet, June 1952. The road on the right is Court Lane. In the 1980s the garage was demolished and in its place the Orchard House apartments were built.

A Durham District bus standing outside the Lord Seaham public house (now the Gilesgate Moor Hotel), Gilesgate Moor, *c.* 1953. The driver is Bill Merrington. Durham District took over the Express Omnibus Company in the early 1950s. The business was started by Mr W. Showler with one Ford car in the 1920s. The garage was at the top of Gilesgate Moor, opposite the Travellers Rest public house.

The Gillet and Baker bus, standing for a posed photograph in Waddington Street, *c.* 1954. The railway viaduct is seen in the top right-hand corner. Gillet & Baker had their garage at Quarrington Hill. The National Bus Company through its subsidiary United Automobile Services Ltd took over Gillet Brothers on 3 November 1974.

Mr Robert Inglis with a dual-purpose United Bus, during the early 1950s. The occasion was a student train-spotting day trip. Mr Inglis ended his working career at the GPO, Providence Row, Durham City, retiring in 1981 on health grounds.

A United bus standing in the old bus station at the top of North Road, May 1968. The station was built in about 1928 and was a cast-iron construction; it was taken down in 1976. The architect was A.H. Fennell and the contractor H.F. Mole, both from Chester-le-Street.

Gradon's lorry standing on Palace Green, *c.* 1946. The firm had its premises at 56 North Road. The business had been established in about 1814 by Forsters; Gradons took over in about 1840, as builders' merchants and monumental masons.

The building of the through road at the top of North Road, *c.* 1970. Here the bulldozer is seen cutting through to link up with the Millburngate Bridge.

The building of Millburngate Bridge and Millburngate House, 1966. The Millburngate Bridge was formally opened on 3 April 1967 by the Chairman of Durham County Council, Councillor S.C. Docking. The bridge was designed by Durham County Council's County Engineer and Surveyor, Mr H.B. Cotton, and County Architect Mr G.W. Gelson. The contractors were Holst & Co. Ltd. The cost of the bridge was £340,000.

The demolition of the second police-box in Durham Market Place, 18 November 1975. Its sole purpose was to direct traffic through the city centre by the manual operation of traffic lights. The police-box was a famous Durham landmark for many years (see page 112 for the first police-box).

Framwellgate Bridge, c. 1964. A swan narrowly avoids danger! It is hard to believe that before 1967 all vehicles, including the emergency services, travelled this route through the city. The bridge was pedestrianized in 1975.

Section Three

RURAL SCENES

Mr Thomas Turner, 1962. Farm hind at Bent
House Farm, Dragonville, Mr Turner was
awarded a long service medal for fifty years'
service. A married farm-servant for whom a
cottage was provided was called a hind in Scottish
and north country dialects.

A charming rural scene in the 1920s; cows walking down Kepier Lane to the farmyard at Kepier. The farmer at the time was Robert Harper. Many older residents still refer to it as Harper's Farm.

A typical farmyard scene at Kepier, 1920s. The farmhouse is a much altered medieval building. The building covered in ivy to the right of the farmhouse in the orchard is possibly part of the medieval hospital buildings.

Kepier Gatehouse, photographed by John Edis, *c.* 1930. This gatehouse was built in about 1333–45 by Bishop Richard de Bury. The style is very similar to the College Gatehouse in the South Bailey.

Hallgarth Water Mill, 1920s. The mill stood on the roadside between Sherburn Village and Pittington. It was here on a hot summer Sunday on 8 August 1830 that Mary Ann Westhorpe, aged seventeen, was murdered by Thomas Clarke, nineteen. Clarke was tried and publicly executed at Durham in front of a crowd of approximately 15,000 spectators. On two other occasions tragedy hit the mill. Ex-police sergeant George Hugill suffered a fatal accident there in May 1923, when he was trapped in the cogs. His predecessor, the owner, was found drowned near the mill.

Shadforth Water Mill in the 1930s. The mill was originally known as Sherburn Mill East. It was a corn mill and was situated in a field called Ox Pasture. One of the earliest references to the mill is in 1605, when it was leased to William Shadforth for twenty-one years. The last occupants were the Crawford family, who left in the 1920s. The remains can still be seen as earthworks on the boundary between Shadforth and Sherburn.

Harvesting time at Bent House Farm, *c.* 1950. The men are seen here cutting hay at Dragon Ville. Left to right: Wilf Stoker, Thomas Turner and Bill Cowling. The field now has a supermarket built upon it. The building on the right was Fowler & Armstrong's garage.

Mr Gowland Collier with his haycart at the top of Church Street near the New Inn, *c.* 1910.

Sheep shearing at Old Durham Farm, May 1915.

Harvesting using the threshing machine at Lowes Barn Farm, *c.* 1920. The farmer at the time was W. Carter.

The Hallgarth Farm building in New Elvet, *c*. 1890. Originally the farm was called Elvet Hall Manor; most of the buildings were medieval. It was once part of the Priory estates and was administered by the hospitaller, the monk responsible for the Priory guests and their accommodation. The medieval tithe barn shown in the centre was threatened with demolition in the late 1960s, when the Prison Department of the Home Office wanted to demolish it to extend prison buildings. It is now the prison officers' club.

The old barn at Hallgarth Farm, 1920s. The buildings on the left were the business premises of A. Broughton, botanical brewer. The business was established in Durham by John Fentiman, son of a Yorkshire brewer, in about 1903. Mr Broughton became the proprietor in about 1908. Later the Fentimans and Broughtons became linked by marriage. The business closed in 1974.

Low Dryburn Farm, North End, *c.* 1920. The occupant at the time was Mr Edward Dixon, who was one of the directors of Pattison's cabinet-making and upholstery business, Elvet Bridge.

High Grange medieval tithe barn, *c.* 1960. It stood near where Gilesgate Junior School is now. This photograph was taken shortly before it was demolished to make way for the new housing estate. William Leech bought the High Grange Estate land from local farmer Mr W. Dixon in December 1959, for £17,537 10s. Many gardens on the High Grange estate salvaged stone for garden rockeries.

William H. Clarkson from Providence Place, Gilesgate Moor, with the milk-cart at Coldknuckles Farm, near Shadforth, *c.* 1906. (Coldknuckles Farm stood near Shadforth Mill – see page 62.)

Joseph March Clarkson with his niece, Mabel Clarkson, and great nephew John Myers, at Providence Place, Gilesgate Moor, about to set out to sell their home produce, *c.* 1914.

Farm labourers burying potatoes for winter storage at Houghall Farm, *c.* 1920. George Tennick is pictured third from the left.

St Cuthbert's Church, built in 1858 by E.R. Robson, seen from Wharton Park, *c.* 1935. The new County Hall building now stands to the right.

Section Four

EDUCATION

*A tree planting ceremony at Whinney Hill School,
1937. Left to right: Mr Thomas Pawson, Mr
George Carpenter and the Marquess of
Londonderry KG, Mayor of Durham.*

Old Durham School, Dragon Villa, 1890s. The school had previously been a military barracks for the Marquess of Londonderry's 2nd Durham Artillery Volunteers. The school still survives in the form of a showroom and cottages named Vane Villas (Sherburn Road).

A class from Old Durham School, c. 1898. Back row, second from the right, is Arthur Clarkson; centre row, second from the right, is Lucy Clarkson; and front row, right, are twins Isaac and Henry Clarkson.

Bede Model School – a classroom scene, *c.* 1900. The model school served as a practice school for the student teachers of Bede College. It closed on 31 August 1933.

Blue Coat Infants at Seaham Hall, 31 August 1911. The occasion was a summer fête given by Lord and Lady Londonderry for the Durham City schoolchildren. Three thousand children and their teachers left Elvet station on four different trains. Each child was presented with a commemorative medal portraying Lord and Lady Londonderry, Mayor and Mayoress of Durham, on one side and on the reverse 'Seaham Hall, August 1911'.

An aerial view showing Durham School, 1930s. To the left you can see St Margaret's allotments. In October 1988 all allotment holders received notice to vacate their plots from the agents acting for the diocese of Durham. It was later revealed that a developer was interested in the land for housing. A successful campaign was launched by the allotment holders to save them from the developers.

St Godric's Roman Catholic School, Castle Chare, 1928. One young boy in the front row is without shoes. This lack of adequate footwear was quite common in the late 1920s, as people were still suffering from the General Strike of 1926.

Teachers from Whinney Hill School, *c.* 1950.

Millburngate Nursery, early 1960s. This was built for the children of munition workers during the Second World War; the site is now occupied by Millburngate Shopping Centre.

Durham Castle (University College) as seen from the upstairs window of Smith the Chemist, Silver Street, *c*. 1936. This picture shows the view obtained when buildings were demolished for the construction of Marks & Spencer's new store. University College was the foundation college of the University of Durham.

St Mary's College, housed in The Cathedral College, *c.* 1921. The building is now The Chorister School. The college was dedicated to St Mary in 1920. The new St Mary's is situated off Quarry Heads Lane; the building was officially started in October 1947 when Princess Elizabeth (the present Queen) laid the foundation stone.

Hatfield Hall, North Bailey, *c.* 1910. Formerly an eighteenth-century coaching inn named the Red Lion, Hatfield became the second college of Durham University in 1846.

Teachers from St Joseph's Roman Catholic School, Mill Lane, Gilesgate Moor, 1963. Back row, left to right: T. Kain, K. Forrester, P. Doran. Front row: M. Dixon, P. Reed, T. Tobin, N. Watson, M. Doyle.

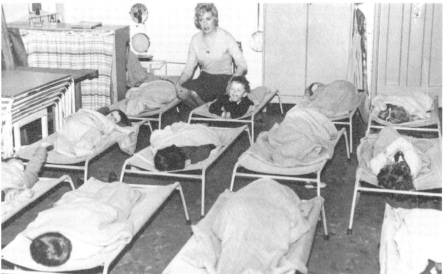

Sheila Rutherford watches over the children at Gilesgate Nursery, which stood near Wood & Watson's car park, *c.* 1965. The nursery established a much-valued afternoon sleeping period for the children. The nursery was similar to Millburngate Nursery (see page 74).

Section Five

INDUSTRY

Two lamp boys from Framwellgate Colliery,

1919. On the left is Joseph Pallister, aged

fourteen, from Smokey Row, Framwellgate Moor,

photographed on his first day down the pit.

Men leaving the Grange Iron Works, Carrville, *c*. 1920. In 1887 at the Royal Exhibition at Newcastle upon Tyne the company was awarded two silver and one bronze medal for their colliery machinery. The iron works at Carrville closed in 1926 when it was amalgamated with Messrs J. Cook, Sons & Co. Ltd of the Washington Steel & Iron Works. The photographer was A. Dunn, South Street, West Rainton.

The yard of the Grange Iron Works, 1914. The iron works had its own gasworks, which produced all the lighting for the works and offices. Many of the buildings and bridges made were in kit form, with each part numbered. Photographs would be taken to help in the erection when the kit reached its destination.

The staff of the Grange Iron Works, *c.* 1916. At that time they were receiving orders from New South Wales, New Zealand, South Africa, China, Brazil, India and other parts of the world.

The turning shop of the Iron Works, 1890s. The Grange Colliery had previously occupied the site.

Kepier Colliery, *c*. 1850. The colliery was owned by Ralph Dixon of 64 Claypath. It was on the site of the present council yard at Glue Garth, Sunderland Road, Gilesgate. The colliery was well under way by 1818; it worked the Hutton & Low main seams. By 1870 the colliery was unproductive, and it was abandoned in 1872. Plans were drawn up by the city council in 1929 to turn the spoil heap into a play area, now known locally as the 'Duff Heap'.

Sherburn Hill Colliery, 1920s. The chimneys on the right belonged to the coke works. The colliery was sunk in 1835, and was closed in August 1965.

Drift-mine workings in Kepier Wood, *c.* 1930. The coal tubs were pulled by steel ropes. The *Durham County Advertiser* of 6 July 1926 reported that John Smith, aged twenty-five, of Claypath, had been trapped by a fall of stone at Kepier Drift. There are still signs of mine-working in Kepier Woods, for example the small stone walls leading into the drifts from the towpaths.

Sherburn House Colliery, 1890s. It was sunk in 1844 and closed in 1932. The colliery was first leased to the Earl of Durham, later Lambton Collieries and later still Lambton and Hetton Collieries. In 1913 Sir B. Samuelson & Company took over the lease, and finally, in 1923, Dorman, Long & Co. The colliery site was opposite Grand View, Sherburn Village.

Miners from Sherburn House Colliery in the 1920s. Left to right: Robert Gainforth, Mr Ormiston and Sammy Bunch. Coal-hewers' wages were approximately *9s 8d* per week in the 1920s.

Easington Colliery band in North Road for the Durham Big Meeting, *c.* 1952. The banner is seen draped in black, which showed that there had been a death in the colliery that year.

Brandon Colliery Prize Silver Band, 1929. The band had a high reputation and was under the direction of Fred Bowes as conductor. In 1934 they competed at the Crystal Palace Tournament. This photograph was taken outside the colliery manager's house.

A miner rests at the Racecourse on the afternoon of the Miners' Gala, *c.* 1950. Pelaw Wood is in the background.

A young boy, holding his bow and arrow, with his mother on the Racecourse at the Durham Miners' Gala, *c.* 1949.

A typical scene on Miners' Gala Day, 1930s. Carters sell their wares. Again, the banners are draped in black (see page 83).

Two miners from one of the colliery villages on the outskirts of the city exercising their dogs, 1930s. On the reverse of the picture the name Bill Routledge appears.

Mr Jack Wilkinson, left, working on an electrical motor at Messrs Hornes and Co., 67 New Elvet, c. 1948. The Durham branch was established in 1913 and specialized in repairing colliery machinery. The firm is now known as Dowding & Mills, and the Durham branch is at Dragon Ville Industrial Estate.

A young-looking Harold Wilson pays a visit to Bickley's Clothing factory, Dragon Ville, in the late 1940s.

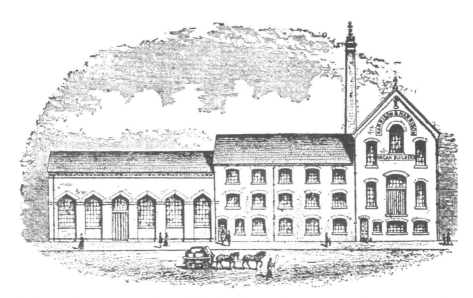

A nineteenth-century engraving of Harrison's organ factory in Hawthorn Terrace. The firm was founded by Thomas Hugh Harrison in Rochdale, Lancashire, in 1861. The factory site in Durham had previously been an old paper mill.

The workforce of Harrison's organ factory, photographed outside the main entrance for the firm's centenary (1861–1961).

Jack Ritchie, the district tuner, Harrison's organ factory, c. 1971.

Gilesgate Soap Works, 42 Gilesgate, 1880s. The Soap Works was established in October 1874 by the Co-operative Wholesale Society. Later, in 1902, the Drill Hall belonging to the 8th Durham Light Infantry was built on the site.

Old Durham Sand Quarry, 1930s. At the beginning of the Second World War a Roman bathhouse was discovered when the Durham City Sand & Gravel Company cut a test pit, with a view to extending the quarry. The Roman bathhouse was of the Antonine period; archaeological digs were carried out, but sadly the remains were lost for ever with the extensive quarrying.

William Coulson Fawcett, c. 1906. He was the last manager of Elvet Colliery. In 1906 he was lowered down a shaft, probably in the river banks, to inspect the flooded workings. His subsequent report led to the closure of the colliery and the loss of his job. He was the grandfather of Councillor William C. Fawcett, former headmaster of Cheveley Park Infant & Junior School,

Hugh Mackay's stand at the North-East Coast Exhibition, 1929. This loom was worked by the Prince of Wales (later Edward VIII) when he visited the exhibition. The rug which was woven at the exhibition was later auctioned for the Durham Castle restoration fund.

Herbert Richardson (the author's great-uncle) working on the carpet shearer at Mackay's, 1929. The shearer removed a fine layer of wool from the pile to give a perfect finish.

Lucy Palmer and Joyce Lightfoot inspecting finished carpets at the factory, *c.* 1950. As far back as the 1920s Mackay's had offices in London, Manchester, Birmingham, Belfast, Glasgow, Melbourne and Sydney.

The factory was partly destroyed in an arson attack by an employee, May 1969. To the left of the picture is Martin's Flour Mill and the ice-rink.

Millburngate and the carpet factory site as seen from the tower of St Margaret's Church, Crossgate, 1920s. The old bridge which crossed the mill-race can be seen to the left of the picture, right of the large chimney. Blagdon's Leather Works are on the left; in the centre is Martin's Flour Mill; and on the right part of Mackay's carpet factory can be seen.

Section Six

LICENSED

PREMISES

Mr James Elliot, landlord of the Sun Inn,

34 Hallgarth Street, c. 1933. Mr Elliot was also a

prison warder at Durham. The Sun Inn is now a

private house. This section is included in Durham at

Work *on the understanding that hard work deserves a*

little relaxation – and the bar staff are workers, too!

Old Elvet, looking towards Elvet Bridge, showing the Waterloo and the County Hotels on the right, 1860s. The County Hotel brickwork is shown before it was plastered over. To the left of the photograph is the old Durham City Working Men's Club, which was previously the Wheatsheaf Inn (see opposite page). Later, in 1897, it became the Royal Mail Inn, and in 1898 the Cycle Hotel.

A close-up view of the Working Men's Club, 2 Old Elvet, *c*. 1904. The property was pulled down in about 1904 and four small retail shops were built on the site (see page 12).

The Pineapple Inn, Old Durham Gardens, *c*. 1910. The landlord at the time was Mr J. Clifford. A public right of way still exists through Old Durham Gardens.

The Tanners' Arms, 48 Framwellgate, 1950s. The public house was situated on the left-hand side going up Framwellgate Peth. The site is now occupied by an open-air car park.

The Blue Bell Inn, 98 Framwellgate, *c.* 1960. It was one of the last properties to be demolished for the new road system in the early 1960s.

The Wearmouth Bridge Hotel, 17 Claypath, 1960s. The old gas showrooms can be seen to the right.

The staff of the Wearmouth Bridge Hotel, 17 Claypath, *c.* 1920.

The Wheatsheaf staff and customers, 17 July 1954. Back row, left to right: Mr and Mrs Burnip, -?-. Front row: Benny Bradley, Minnie Snowdon.

A Leek Club party at the Wheatsheaf, 3 Claypath, *c*. 1958.

The Rose & Crown Hotel, Market Place (now Woolworths) decorated for the Diamond Jubilee of Queen Victoria, 1897. The manager William MacFarlane and his staff can be seen on the left. The Rose & Crown had a history going back to 1633, when Charles I was presented with silver plate there by the Freemen of the City.

The Royal Hotel, Co-operative Terrace, 1960s. This area was demolished to make way for the through road from Millburngate to the top of North Road.

The Railway Hotel, which stood to the right of the Royal Hotel, 1960s. This was demolished at the same time as the Royal Hotel, for the new through road.

The King's Arms Hotel, 105 Claypath, 1960s. This building stood to the left of what is now Boots the Chemist, along with many other shops. These were demolished in the early 1960s for the new through road.

The Station Hotel, which stood at the top of North Road, 1960s. It also had to make way for the through road.

The Market Hotel, Market Place, 1919. The small white sign in the window reads 'No Ladies Supplied'. It was here on 20 November 1869 that the Durham Miners' Association was formed.

Mr Robert Robertson, landlord, standing outside the old Woodman Inn, 23 Gilesgate, *c*. 1920. It was pulled down and rebuilt in the 1920s. This building dated from the early eighteenth century. A stone lintel from the old inn was placed above the new back door; it reads 'G.M. 1715'.

The Maltman Hotel, 29 Claypath, 1960s. The building is now Heron's cycle shop. To the left is the old Palladium cinema, which was built and owned by the Holliday family. The cinema has stood empty for many years; it was last used as a bingo hall.

New Durham Working Men's Club's first Leek Show, September 1958. Left to right: Mr R. Gleason, Harry Wills, -?-, Bob Fairless, -?-, Jack Mollon, Bill Hann, Tommy Thompson. Jack Mollon was the first gardener to win the New Durham and District Club Leek Trophy.

The old Three Horse Shoes, 16 Sunderland Road, *c*. 1920. To the right of the building is the old Coach Opening, which got its name from the Railway Coach – a name previously given to the Three Horse Shoes.

The Bay Horse Inn, 110 Gilesgate, in the 1930s. It has now been rebuilt and renamed the Durham Light Infantryman. Behind the Bay Horse stood Lockerbie's shoeing forge (see page 22).

The old Hare & Hounds, 39 Sunderland Road, early 1960s. To the left can be seen the building of the present-day Hare & Hounds. Left to right: Tommy Dance, Joe Barker and the landlord, Matty Cooper.

The Bay Horse Inn, West Sherburn, *c.* 1910. The landlord, Edwin Bamlett, is standing in the doorway. The inn is now known as The Tavern. The old road to Sherburn once passed the inn before the new motorway bridge was built in the 1960s.

The Grange Inn, Carrville, named after the nearby Grange Iron Works, *c.* 1924. The photograph shows Evelyn, Jack and William, the children of the landlord, William Graymorrow.

DEFENCE OF THE REALM

*Bugler Walter Shea, proudly wearing his
dress uniform of the 8th Durham Light
Infantry (Territorials), c. 1922. Walter
spent all his working life at Mackay's Carpet
Factory. He also wrote the history of
Carpet-Making in Durham City.*

Sergeants of the 2nd North Durham Militia, standing outside the main door of the Militia Barracks (now Vane Tempest Hall), *c.* 1874. The barracks were built in 1864; the militia had previously had their headquarters in Church Street, opposite St Oswald's Church.

Sergeant Thomas Beeby, *c.* 1901. Born in Gilesgate, he was a groom when he joined the 4th Durham Light Infantry (Militia) in 1887, aged nineteen. He soon rose to the rank of sergeant and served in the Boer War, attached to the 3rd Durham Light Infantry (Militia). In 1901 he was awarded the DCM, the only soldier from the 4th Durham Light Infantry to receive this medal. He died in Sherburn House Hospital in July 1910, from tuberculosis.

An official 'Welcome Home' reception, marching down North Road in the direction of Framwellgate Bridge, *c.* 1919. The King William public house stands on the right. The officer leading centre (of the front row) is Colonel Turnbull of the 8th Battalion Durham Light Infantry.

The 5th Durham Voluntary Aid Hospital (VAH), in the North Bailey (now Cranmer Hall), *c.* 1915. Many of the first Voluntary Aid Detachment (VAD) members were former suffragettes. The gentleman with his arm bandaged is Joseph Pattison of Ivy Cottage, near Brown's Boat House.

'B' Company, Durham Royal Garrison Artillery, during the First World War. They are seen here at the Barracks, Gilesgate (Vane Tempest Hall). In December 1931 the barracks were put up for sale by auction by Mr J.W. Wood, on behalf of the owner, the Marquess of Londonderry.

The First World War tank in Wharton Park, c. 1926. The tank was presented by the National War Savings Association in appreciation of local efforts. On 10 June 1919 it arrived at Gilesgate Goods station. Tank No. 2783 was one of the original tanks to be used in the First World War; it first saw action at Vimy Ridge and later at Arras. It was officially handed over to the city at Wharton Park on 17 June 1919.

'B' Squadron, Northumberland Hussars, Rifle Team, *c.* 1927. 'B' Squadron were based at the Barracks (Vane Tempest Hall). Most of the men were local, and in the 1920s they had a waiting list of 100 young men waiting to join. The photograph shows the winners of the Territorial Army Rifle Associations Competitions 1926–27. Top row, left to right: Tprs. T.D. Thompson, A. Saborn, L/Cpl. J. Brice, Tpr J.P. Nichol. Middle row: Tprs. G.W. Lightburn, W. Allison, R.O. Sutton, T. Stoddart, M. Blackburn, J. Harris, E. Geary, W. Dunmore, A. Sharp. Front row: Farrier E. Shepherd, L/Sgt. C. Roberts, F/Sgt. W. Telford, S.S.M. H. Lee, Capt. C. Vaux. M.C. (Squadron Leader), Sgt. W.H. Crees (PSI), Sgts. T. Halliday, M. Thompson, L/Cpl. A. Baldwin.

PC Dick Collinson on duty in the first police-box, 1940. It is interesting to see the war-time issue tin helmet. This police-box appeared in the early 1930s, and became a landmark in the city. It was demolished in 1957 and was replaced by the second police-box (see page 58).

(see page 58)

ARP (Air Raid Precautions) Wardens on duty at Gilesgate, *c.* 1942. The photograph was taken in the grounds of the old 'Gate' School, which became St Giles' church hall (St Giles' filling station is built on the site). The warden in the middle is Mr Tom Robinson, of 1 Malvern Terrace, Gilesgate.

Durham City Auxiliary Fire Service, *c.* 1940. The photograph was taken on the Sands, at the bottom of Providence Row. Top row, left to right: Firemen ? Bunker, J. Green, B. Hammill, M. Carrol. Front row: B. Blakey, J. Armstrong, T. Clish, W. Wills, Colonel Officer J. Willis, G. Shannon, Leading Fireman C. Brown and Section Leader N. Murray.

Durham City Observer Corps, 14 December 1944. The headquarters stood behind the old post office in Providence Row. Top row, left to right: Betty Newby, Enid Garnham. Middle row: Margery Gavin, Mary Morrison. Front row: Nora Weavers, Dorothy Meade, Betty MacIntyre, Rhona Robson, Irene Richardson, Daisy Armstrong and Mona Taylor.

The 8th Durham Light Infantry, Pioneer Corp, British Expeditionary Force, 1940. The soldier behind the axes in the centre is Tommy Bond (Pioneer Sergeant).

Durham City Home Guard on the steps of Durham Castle, *c.* 1945.

A royal visit to Durham Castle during the Second World War, *c.* 1943. King George and Queen Elizabeth are seen leaving.

Neville's Cross students, who were transferred to Bede College at the beginning of the Second World War, seen entering the air raid shelter, *c.* 1940. Neville's Cross College was taken over by the War Office as a casualty clearing station.

Regimental Bicentenary Parade, 17 May 1958. The Flag's colour party is seen marching towards the entrance of the old Drill Hall (home of the 8th Battalion Durham Light Infantry) at the bottom of Gilesgate Bank. The Drill Hall was officially opened on 7 February 1902. It was built by Messrs Jasper Kell & Sons, North Road, Durham City; the architect was J. Oswald & Son, of Newcastle.

Territorials from the 8th Battalion Durham Light Infantry walking back from the Cathedral after an Armistice Parade at the Cathedral, 1974. Leading the parade is Major J. Jackson, followed by Captain Robinson and Colour-Sergeant Major C. Armstrong.

VE day party at the Duck Pond, Gilesgate, 8 May 1945. The building in the background is Gilesgate Methodist Church. The young child sitting on a woman's knee in the front row on the left is Doretta Savage, the author's mother.

DURHAM AT PRAYER

Bishop Hensley Henson, photographed by John Edis,
c. 1929. Dean of Durham 1913–18; Bishop of Hereford
1918–20; Bishop of Durham 1920–39. His consecration
had been strongly opposed by Anglo-Catholics. As Bishop
of Durham he became increasingly liberal in his
churchmanship, and took a notable part in national
ecclesiastical conflicts.

The burnt-out ruins of Sherburn Hospital Chapel after the fire, December 1864. The Revd J. Carr, Master of the Hospital, had banked up the fire on the evening of Saturday 3 December to warm the church for Sunday, but the flue had become blocked; wood panelling caught fire in the early hours of Sunday morning.

The Congregational Chapel,
Claypath, c. 1880. This building still
survives, tucked away behind the
United Reformed Church.

A typical Durham house, 1885.
This house, 48 Claypath, was the
residence of Alfred Tucker when he
was curate of St Nicholas' Church.
He later went on to become the
first Bishop of Uganda,
1899–1911.

An unusual view of St Margaret's Church, Crossgate, in the 1890s. The church dates
from around 1160. The font is twelfth-century and is of Frosterley Marble. Originally
part of St Oswald's parish, this church served the residents of the Borough of Crossgate.
Burials were not permitted here until 1431. Sir John Duck, the Durham Dick
Whittington, is buried here along with members of the Shafto family.

The remains of the old Wesleyan Chapel, Rotten Row (Court Lane), 1920s. It was here that John Wesley preached on a number of occasions when he visited Durham. The chapel was established in 1770. The building was demolished in the 1940s. In 1808 a new chapel was built in Chapel Passage, Old Elvet, and in 1904 the Elvet Methodist Church was built.

St Hild's Chapel, *c.* 1913. It is rarely seen, as it is tucked away in the grounds of St Hild's College surrounded by student accommodation. The chapel is now, sadly, used for storage. It was built by John Shepherd of Gilesgate, and was dedicated on 14 June 1913.

Harvest Festival, Houghall Mission, 1920s. This corrugated iron building was in the parish of St Oswald's. It served the small community of Houghall, which at one time was a thriving mining village.

The congregation of the Jubilee Primitive Methodist Chapel at the centenary celebrations of the founding of the society (1824–1924) at Wharton Park.

The Jubilee Primitive Methodist Chapel, North Road, *c.* 1961. The Iceland freezer shop now occupies this site. On 19 May 1861 the Jubilee Church was opened. Before that date the congregation had been meeting in a small chapel in Back Silver Street.

An early engraving of St Giles' Church, 1824. It was drawn by Joseph Bouet (1791–1856), the French artist who taught art and French at Durham School.

Acknowledgements

So many people have donated photographs to the Gilesgate Archive that it is impossible to thank them individually. Institutions which have helped include:

Durham University Library, Palace Green; Durham City Reference Library; Durham Arts, Libraries & Museums Department; Durham County Council; the trustees of the Durham Light Infantry Museum.

Without this assistance this book would never have been possible and the author acknowledges it gratefully. If any reader has new material or information, it would be helpful if contact could be made with:

Michael Richardson, 128 Gilesgate, Durham DH1 1QG (0191–384–1427).